THE PHASES OF THE MOON

Suzanne Slade

The Rosen Publishing Group's
PowerKids Press™
New York

To Mrs. Valerie Plebanski—a special kind of teacher who comes along once in a blue moon

Published in 2007 by the Rosen Publishing Group, Inc.
29 East 21st Street, New York, NY 10010

First Edition

Editor: Joanne Randolph
Book Design: Greg Tucker
Photo Researcher: Amy Feinberg

Photo Credits: Cover © PhotoDisc; pp. 4, 6, 8, 10, 12, 14, 16, 18, 20 Greg Tucker; p. 5 © Theo Allofs/Corbis; p. 7 © Tom Bullock/www.tombullock.com; p. 9 © Frank Lukasseck/zefa/Corbis; p. 11 Courtesy NASA-JPL; p. 13 (left) © Franz-Marc Frei/Corbis; p. 13 (right) © Free Agents Limited/Corbis; pp. 15, 19, 21 (bottom) © Roger Ressmeyer/Corbis; p. 17 © Jeff Vanuga/Corbis; p. 21 (top) © Corbis.

Library of Congress Cataloging-in-Publication Data

Slade, Suzanne.
  The phases of the moon / Suzanne Slade.— 1st ed.
     p. cm. — (Cycles in nature)
  Includes index.
  ISBN 1-4042-3488-8 (library binding) — ISBN 1-4042-2197-2 (pbk.) — ISBN 1-4042-2387-8 (six pack)
  1. Moon—Juvenile literature. I. Title. II. Cycles in nature (PowerKids Press)
  QB582.S549 2007
  523.3'2—dc22
                                    2005029495

Manufactured in the United States of America

Contents

Phases of the Moon

The shape of the Moon changes every night. Sometimes it is full and round. Other nights it is thin and curved. The different appearances of the Moon are called **phases**. These phases are caused by the movement of the Moon.

The Moon moves in a circle around, or orbits, **planet** Earth. The Moon is Earth's only natural **satellite**. Half of the Moon's surface is always lit up by the Sun. As the Moon orbits Earth, you can see a different part of the sunlit half of the Moon every night. The Moon

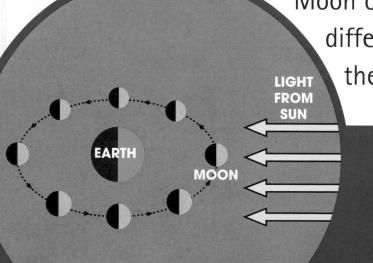

LIGHT
FROM
SUN

EARTH

MOON

This diagram shows the lunar cycle. One-half of the Moon is always lit up by the Sun. From Earth the Moon's shape appears different every night. This happens because we see different amounts of the Moon's surface as it orbits Earth.

makes a complete circle around Earth, called a revolution, in about 28 days. Most months are 30 or 31 days long, so you can see a complete **cycle** of the phases of the Moon every month.

A full moon rises over the mountaintops at Mount Torre in Argentina.

Cycle Facts

The word "lunar" comes from the Latin word for "moon," *luna*. After the Sun the Moon is the second-brightest object we see in the sky.

New Moon

There are eight phases of the Moon. The first phase is the new moon. The interesting thing about the new moon is that you cannot see it! During a new moon, the Moon is located between the Sun and Earth. All the Moon's lit side is toward the Sun. The side of the Moon facing Earth is completely dark. Although you cannot see the new moon, it is easy to observe the Moon's other phases. Earth's **gravity** keeps the Moon close. The Moon is

LIGHT FROM SUN

EARTH

MOON

The Moon appears dark during the new moon, because the Moon sits directly between the Sun and Earth. This means that we cannot see the part of the Moon that is lit.

about 250,000 miles (402,336 km) from Earth. You can also see the Moon because it is so large. The Moon measures 2,160 miles (3,476 km) across. It is one-fourth the size of Earth.

This special picture shows the phases of the Moon. There appear to be only seven phases here, because we cannot see the new moon.

Cycle Facts

Although Earth has only one moon, other planets have several moons. For example, Mars has two moons. Saturn has 50 moons and Jupiter has 63 known moons. Earth's moon is the fifth- largest moon of the different planets in our solar system.

Waxing Crescent

The Moon's second phase is called the waxing crescent. It appears one or two days after the new moon. The word "crescent" means "shaped like a C." A waxing crescent moon is small and thin and looks like a backward letter C. "Waxing" means "to get bigger." The Moon gets a little bigger every night until it is a full circle. If you watch the sky closely, you will see the waxing crescent moon first appear during the daytime.

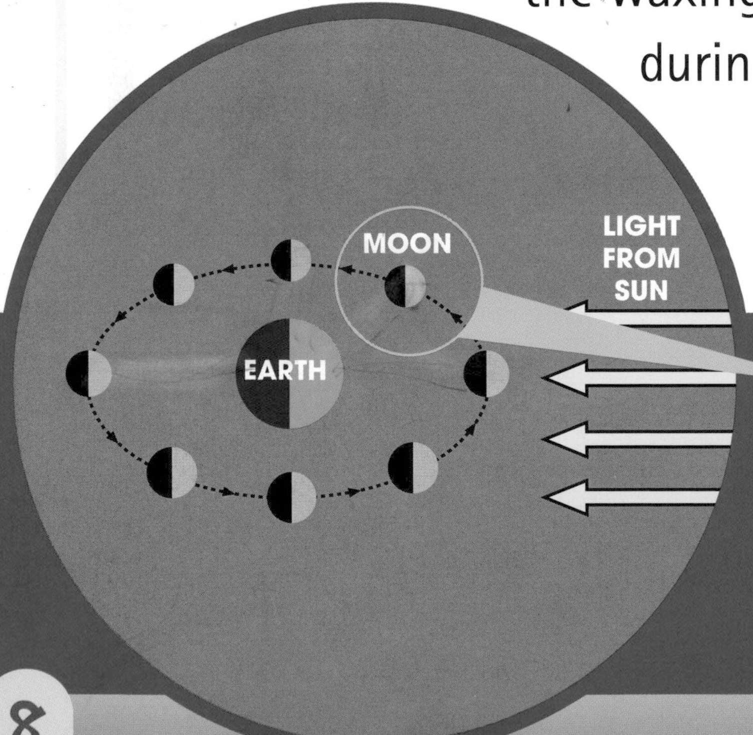

MOON

LIGHT FROM SUN

EARTH

As the Moon continues to move around Earth, we begin to see a small part of it.

Earth's day is 24 hours long. Daytime is what we call the part of the day during which we get sunlight. Earth is turned away from the Sun during the rest of the 24-hour day. Night is what we call those hours of darkness. The Moon's day is about one month long. Day and night on the Moon each last for about two weeks.

The waxing crescent starts out very thin and grows larger until it reaches the next phase.

Cycle Facts

If you want to see how the lunar cycle works, you can try an experiment. Place a round object on a table to stand for Earth. Use another round object to stand for the Moon. Have a friend shine a flashlight from one side to stand for the Sun. Now move the moon around the object on the table, and watch the cycle of your moon.

First Quarter

About seven days after the new moon, the third phase of the Moon appears. The right half of the Moon shines brightly during this phase, called the first quarter. The Moon has finished the first quarter, or one-fourth, of its trip around Earth. Sometimes people call this phase a half-moon because half of the Moon's surface that faces Earth is lit up by the Sun. One side of the Moon always faces Earth. This is called the near side. The side of

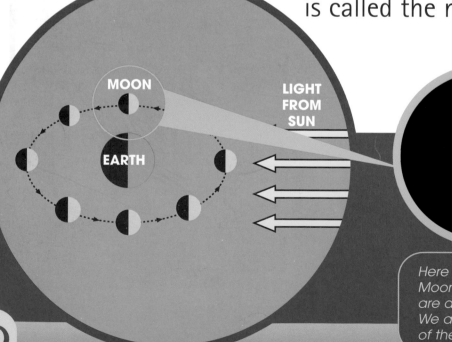

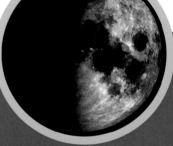

Here you can see where the Moon, the Sun, and the Earth are during the first quarter moon. We are able to see one-quarter of the Moon's surface.

the Moon turned away from Earth is called the far side. The Moon also rotates, or turns, as it orbits Earth. It takes the same amount of time for the Moon to rotate as it does to orbit Earth. Therefore, the same side of the Moon always faces Earth.

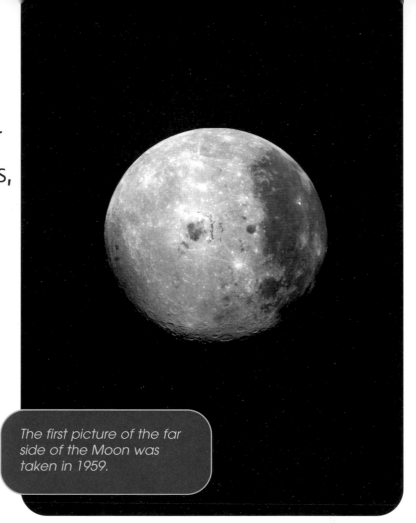

The first picture of the far side of the Moon was taken in 1959.

Cycle Facts

Scientists got their first look at the far side of the Moon when a spacecraft named *Luna 3* sent pictures back to Earth in 1959. The spacecraft called *Luna Prospector* found ice on the far side of the Moon in 1998. That was when scientists first discovered there is water on the Moon.

Waxing Gibbous

As the Moon continues around Earth, the amount of the sunlit half you can see gets larger. A few days after the first quarter, the Moon starts to look like an oval. This phase is called waxing gibbous. "Waxing" means "to grow larger." "Gibbous" means "an oval shape."

Like Earth the Moon has gravity. As the Moon moves across the sky, its gravity pulls on Earth's oceans and causes tides. A tide is the rising

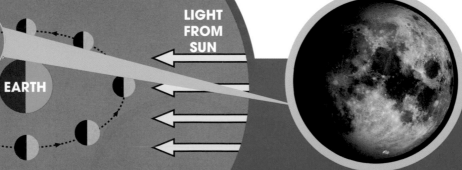

MOON

EARTH

LIGHT FROM SUN

The fourth phase of the Moon is the waxing gibbous phase, shown here. We can see more than half of the Moon's surface during this phase.

or lowering of water. Oceans near the Moon rise because water is pulled to one area by the Moon's gravity. This is called a high tide. As water gathers in high-tide areas, other parts of the ocean have less water. These areas have a low tide.

These two pictures show Mont St. Michel in France. This church sits on a raised piece of land. It gets surrounded by water during high tides and has dry land around it during low tides. The Moon causes the two tides each day.

Cycle Facts

The gravity on the surface of the Moon is much less than Earth's surface gravity. If you weigh 80 pounds (36 kg) on Earth, you would weigh only 13 pounds (6 kg) on the Moon.

Full Moon

The fifth phase of the Moon is a full moon. A full moon looks like a complete circle of light because you see the entire half of the Moon that is lit up by the Sun. The Moon does not create its own light. It **reflects** the light it gets from the Sun. Some full moons provide enough light on Earth to create dim shadows. The Moon reflects only seven **percent** of the sunlight that hits it. Sometimes there are two full moons in one month. The second

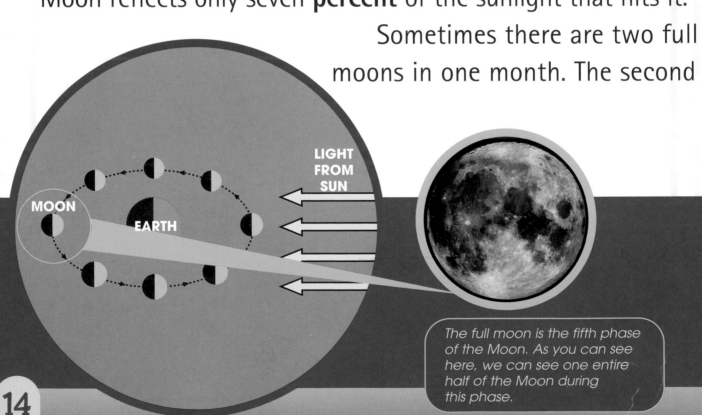

MOON

EARTH

LIGHT FROM SUN

The full moon is the fifth phase of the Moon. As you can see here, we can see one entire half of the Moon during this phase.

A full moon shines above Cuba here. Did you know that the only time a lunar eclipse can happen is during a full moon? The Moon can pass through Earth's shadow during this phase.

full moon is called a blue moon. A blue moon is not blue at all. It is usually yellow or white. Blue moons do not happen very often. People say, "once in a blue moon" when they mean "not very often."

Cycle Facts

Although most people think the Moon is round, it is actually shaped like an egg. The smaller end of the Moon is closer to Earth.

Waning Gibbous

Following a full moon, the Moon starts to wane. "To wane" means "to become smaller." The sixth phase is called waning gibbous. During waning gibbous the left part of the Moon is lit up in an oval shape.

A large part of the Moon's surface is lit up in the waning gibbous phase. If you look closely, you can see large, dark areas on the Moon. These areas are called maria. Maria are flat areas

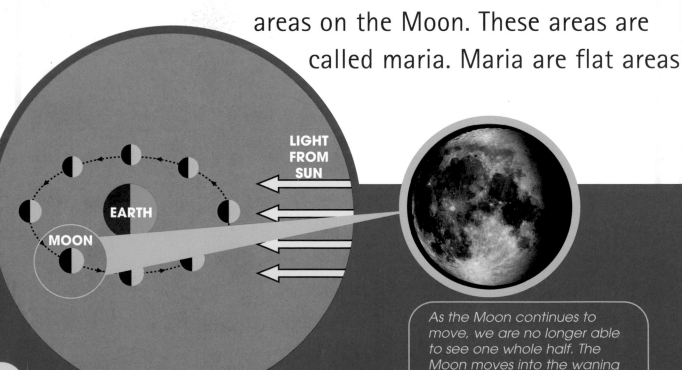

LIGHT FROM SUN

EARTH

MOON

As the Moon continues to move, we are no longer able to see one whole half. The Moon moves into the waning gibbous phase, as shown here.

that are hundreds of miles (km) wide. From Earth maria look like lakes or oceans. Maria are actually covered with a fine, gray dust called regolith. The rest of the Moon's surface is covered with regolith, too. You may also see **craters** on the Moon. Craters are formed when meteorites crash into the Moon. Meteorites are large rocks that float in space.

The position of Earth and the Moon control the time you see the Moon rise each night. You can see this waning gibbous moon even though it is still daytime.

Cycle Facts

The largest crater on the Moon is 1,398 miles (2,250 km) wide and 7 miles (11 km) deep. This crater, named South Pole-Aitken, is located on the far side of the Moon.

Last Quarter

Seven days after the full moon, the seventh phase will appear. This is called the last quarter moon. The left half of the Moon is lit up during the last quarter. Some people call this a half-moon because they see a half circle lit up.

The Moon does not have an **atmosphere**, as Earth does. An atmosphere is a mix of different gases that surrounds a planet. Earth's atmosphere blocks some of the Sun's strong and harmful rays.

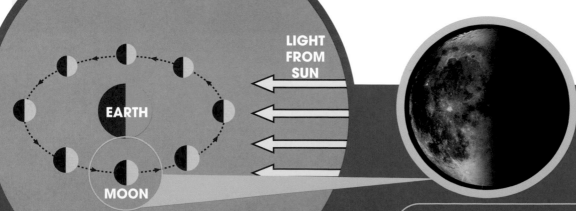

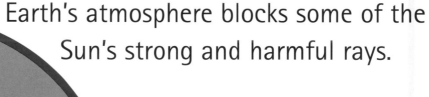

LIGHT FROM SUN

EARTH

MOON

Here you can see where the Moon is in relation to the Sun and Earth during the last quarter. During the last quarter moon, we see the side of the Moon. One-half looks dark and half is lit up by sunlight.

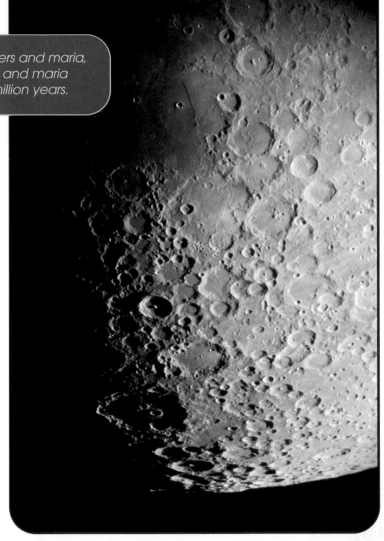

The Moon's surface is covered in craters and maria, as shown here. Many of these craters and maria have been there for more than 100 million years.

Without an atmosphere the Moon's **temperature** gets as high as 225° F (107° C). An atmosphere also holds heat near a planet at night. Temperatures on the Moon get as low as -243° F (-153° C) at night.

Cycle Facts

An atmosphere also creates weather, which can wear away the surface of a planet. The Moon has no wind or rain because it does not have an atmosphere. This means that the surface of the Moon has stayed almost the same for millions of years. The only changes are caused by meteorites.

Waning Crescent

The eighth phase of the Moon is the waning crescent. The Moon continues to wane, or get smaller, and becomes a thin crescent shape. The left side of the Moon is lit up during the waning crescent phase, so it looks like a *C*. The Moon has almost finished its 28-day trip around Earth. Soon the new moon will return, and the Moon will begin its cycle again.

Throughout history people have been curious about the Moon.

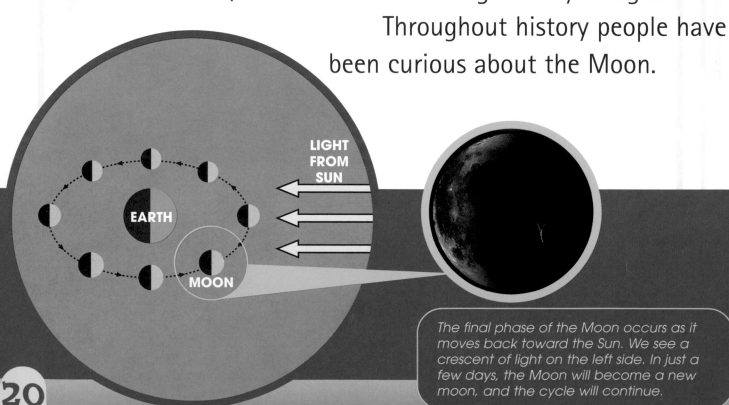

LIGHT FROM SUN

EARTH

MOON

The final phase of the Moon occurs as it moves back toward the Sun. We see a crescent of light on the left side. In just a few days, the Moon will become a new moon, and the cycle will continue.

In 1969, Neil Armstrong became the first **astronaut** to walk on the Moon. His footprints are still there, as is the American flag he placed in the ground. If you were ever to go to the Moon, what would you leave for the next visitor?

This photo shows James Irwin standing on the Moon in 1971. Neil Armstrong was the first person to stand on the Moon's surface in 1969. The first moon landing was a historic event that led the way for the many discoveries in space that followed.

Shown here is a piece of moon rock that was brought back by astronauts. The rock is basalt. Basalt is an igneous rock, which is a kind of rock formed by a great amount of heat.

Cycle Facts

Astronauts have brought back 842 pounds (382 kg) of rocks and dirt from the Moon. By studying these rocks, scientists have learned that the Moon was formed about 4.5 billion years ago.

Eclipses

A **lunar eclipse** occurs when Earth is between the Sun and the Moon. During a lunar eclipse, Earth blocks the Sun's light from reaching the Moon. The entire surface of the Moon is dark.

When the Moon lines up exactly between the Sun and Earth, this is called a **solar** eclipse. During a solar eclipse, the Moon blocks the Sun's rays from hitting Earth. Although the Sun is 400 times larger than the Moon, the Moon is 400 times closer to Earth than the Sun is, so the Moon perfectly blocks the Sun's light from Earth.

Earth's closest neighbor, the Moon, makes a beautiful changing light in Earth's night sky. The next time you look up at the Moon notice its shape. Can you recognize the Moon's phase in the lunar cycle? Which phase of the lunar cycle is it in tonight?

Cycle Facts

The Sun's rays can harm your eyes. You should never look directly at the Sun, even during a solar eclipse.

Glossary

astronaut (AS-truh-not) A person who is trained to travel in outer space.

atmosphere (AT-muh-sfeer) The gases around an object in space. On Earth this is air.

craters (KRAY-turz) Large holes on a moon or a planet.

cycle (SY-kul) A course of events that happens in the same order over and over.

eclipse (ih-KLIPS) A darkening of the Sun or the Moon that occurs when the light of the Sun is blocked by the Moon or when the light of the Moon is blocked by Earth's shadow.

gravity (GRA-vih-tee) The natural force that causes objects to move toward the center of Earth or another body.

lunar (LOO-ner) Of or about the Moon.

percent (pur-SENT) One part of 100.

phases (FAYZ-ez) The different stages of the Moon as seen from Earth.

planet (PLA-net) A large object, such as Earth, that moves around the Sun.

reflects (rih-FLEKTS) Throws back light, heat, or sound.

satellite (SA-tih-lyt) A natural object that circles a planet in space.

solar (SOH-ler) Having to do with the Sun.

temperature (TEM-pur-cher) How hot or cold something is.

Index

Web Sites

Due to the changing nature of Internet links, PowerKids Press has developed an online list of Web sites related to the subject of this book. This site is updated regularly. Please use this link to access the list:
www.powerkidslinks.com/cin/lunar/